NATIONAL GEOGRAPHIC

Ladders

Explorer Tim Samaras

TORNADOES

TWISTER

by Christopher Siegel

"**DO YOU GO TO A WINDOW WHEN YOU HEAR A CLAP OF THUNDER, OR POUNDING RAIN, OR SEE A STREAK OF LIGHTNING IN THE SKY? ME TOO. EXCEPT I TAKE MY CURIOSITY A LITTLE BIT FURTHER. I GO OUT AND CHASE THE BIGGEST STORMS I CAN FIND.**"

The quote above was from Tim Samaras. Tim's curiosity led him to follow some of the worst storms and tornadoes in recent history. He spent over half his life running into the path of tornadoes. He placed research tools in the right places to gather information. He fought powerful winds and rain, chunks of hail, and the scary noise of a racing tornado. He even saw a community destroyed. Tim was a severe storms researcher and a National Geographic Explorer.

Tim put himself in harm's way for science. His goal was to answer questions that will help people better prepare for tornadoes.

TIM SAMARAS was the lead storm researcher for TWISTEX, or Tactical Weather Instrumented Sampling in or near Tornadoes Experiment. He used Science, technology, engineering, and math skills to research tornadoes. Tim hoped that by better understanding tornadoes he could make more accurate predictions and help people prepare for when a tornado strikes.

Tornadoes are some of the most violent storms. They often form from powerful thunderstorms. They can create massive damage.

HOW A TORNADO FORMS

Tornadoes are funnel-shaped clouds of spinning, rising air. They form when warm, wet air quickly rises from the ground. This is called an **updraft.** At the same time, a powerful **downdraft** of cooler air pushes rain and hail to the ground. The warm air and cool air wrap around each other. This creates a swirling funnel of air. The tornado forms when the spinning funnel of air touches the ground.

1.

Warm and cold air usually move in different directions and at different speeds. When they come together, a horizontal tube of air begins to spin.

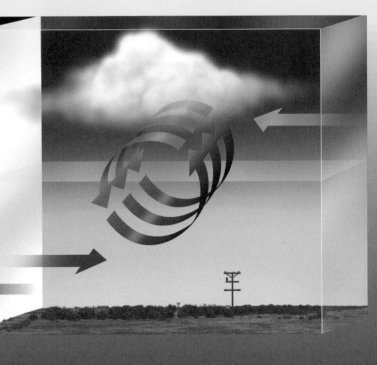

2.

The spinning tube of air begins to tilt upright. The warm air begins to move upward in an updraft. The cooler air flows down in a downdraft. It usually brings rain and hail.

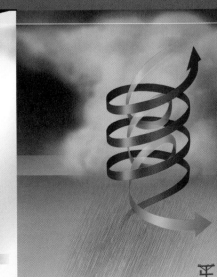

3.

The warm and cold air currents continue to spiral. The rotating winds create a funnel shape. The spiraling funnel becomes a tornado when it touches the ground. The funnel shape can be seen when the tornado picks up debris from the ground.

TORNADO TYPES

All tornadoes have one common characteristic. They are visible to us as funnels that carry debris, water, or other material picked up from where they touched down. The type of debris and material taken up by the tornadoes gives the funnel clouds different colors and shapes. Here are some different tornadoes.

SUPERCELL: This powerful tornado comes out of a **supercell** thunderstorm. The funnel that touches down is often wedge-shaped. Supercells can stay on the ground for a long time and often cause a lot of damage.

WATERSPOUT: A waterspout forms over the surface of a body of water. Waterspouts are usually less powerful and cause less damage than other tornadoes since they occur over water. Waterspouts usually break up once they reach land. However, if they move inland, they can cause a lot of damage and injuries.

FIRE WHIRL: Fire whirls, or fire devils, can form over a forest fire or volcanic eruption. Fire whirls are rotating columns of smoke and fire.

TORNADO ALLEY

More tornadoes touch down in the United States than any other place in the world. Tornadoes can happen anywhere in the U.S., but they are most likely to occur in an area of the central U.S. known as Tornado Alley. The physical geography and environment of Tornado Alley provide the perfect conditions for tornadoes to form.

Tornadoes occur when warm air from the Gulf of Mexico moves north over Tornado Alley. At the same time, cold air from the Rocky Mountains blows south into the area. When the warm and cold air meet, the **atmosphere** becomes unstable. The atmosphere is the layer of air and other gases above Earth. Storm clouds form and the sky darkens. The wind blows stronger. Then hail and rain beat down. The growing storm could easily turn into a tornado.

A TORNADO IN OKLAHOMA ONCE DESTROYED A MOTEL. PEOPLE LATER FOUND THE MOTEL'S SIGN IN ARKANSAS.

IN 1928, A TORNADO IN KANSAS PLUCKED THE FEATHERS RIGHT OFF SOME CHICKENS.

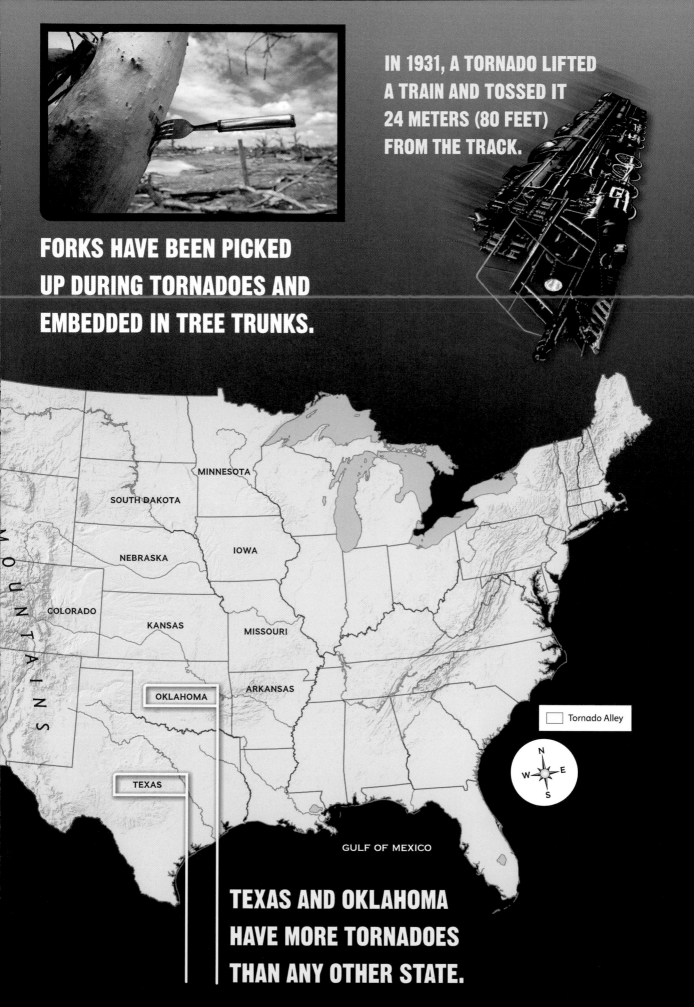

IN 1931, A TORNADO LIFTED
A TRAIN AND TOSSED IT
24 METERS (80 FEET)
FROM THE TRACK.

FORKS HAVE BEEN PICKED
UP DURING TORNADOES AND
EMBEDDED IN TREE TRUNKS.

MINNESOTA

SOUTH DAKOTA

NEBRASKA

IOWA

COLORADO

KANSAS

MISSOURI

ARKANSAS

OKLAHOMA

TEXAS

M O U N T A I N S

Tornado Alley

N
W E
S

GULF OF MEXICO

TEXAS AND OKLAHOMA
HAVE MORE TORNADOES
THAN ANY OTHER STATE.

TORNADO RATINGS

The most violent tornadoes have wind speeds over 322 kilometers per hour (200 miles per hour). They can destroy large buildings, uproot trees, and throw vehicles hundreds of meters.

Scientists and engineers categorize tornadoes using the Enhanced Fujita (EF) Tornado Intensity Scale. Ratings are from EF0 to EF5. The ratings scale is based on the **velocity**, or the speed and direction of the wind, and the kind of damage that occurs.

EF 0

WIND SPEED: 137 km/h (85 mph) or less

LIGHT DAMAGE: small tree branches broken; minor damage to the roofs of houses

EF 1

WIND SPEED: 138–178 km/h (86–110 mph)

MODERATE DAMAGE: windows broken; mobile homes pushed off their bases or flipped over; trees uprooted

EF 2

WIND SPEED: 179–218 km/h (111–135 mph)

CONSIDERABLE DAMAGE: pieces of roof ripped off houses and other buildings; mobile homes destroyed; wooden electrical poles broken

EF 3

WIND SPEED:
219–266 km/h
(136–165 mph)

SEVERE DAMAGE:
walls of houses, schools, and malls toppled; steel electrical poles bent or broken

EF 4

WIND SPEED:
267–322 km/h
(166–200 mph)

DEVASTATING DAMAGE:
houses destroyed; large sections of schools, malls, and other large buildings damaged

EF 5

WIND SPEED:
over 322 km/h
(200 mph)

INCREDIBLE DAMAGE:
schools, malls, high-rise buildings, and other large buildings destroyed

ENHANCED FUJITA (EF)

Tetsuya Theodore Fujita was born in Japan where tornadoes rarely form. Fujita, or "Mr. Tornado," is thought to be one of the world's most famous tornado experts. Fujita originally developed a system in which tornado ratings were only based on the damage that occurred. Later tornado researchers added wind speed to the scale. Fujita's name is used in rating a tornado. "EF" stands for "Enhanced Fujita."

EYEWITNESS TO A Tornado

Compiled by Lara Winegar

On Sunday, May 22, 2011, the Tactical Weather Instrumented Sampling in or near Tornadoes Experiment (TWISTEX) team was chasing a severe thunderstorm just south of Joplin, Missouri. Soon a tornado descended from the **supercell** and was plowing through Joplin. It was one of the deadliest tornadoes to hit the United States in decades.

"The supercell I saw moving across the sky was enormous, and I knew this was a dangerous storm. As the team and I jumped into action to deploy our instruments, I hoped that people in the nearby areas were taking shelter. We sure did, as soon as we possibly could. What follows are some stories from people who experienced this storm."
TIM SAMARAS

Tim Samaras prepares his research equipment before leaving on a storm chase.

> "They were the darkest clouds I've ever seen. All we wanted to do was get home." EMMA COX

Emma Cox

Emma Cox, 17, and her older brother were driving home from his high school graduation. She looked out the windshield and saw low-hanging clouds. She heard tornado sirens whining. Rain beat on the windows and wind rocked the car. Emma and her brother couldn't see anything, not even the brake lights of cars in front of them. She cracked her window open. They heard a spooky whistling sound.

"We didn't realize it at the time," she says, **"BUT IT WAS THE TRAIN WHISTLE SOUND THAT EVERYONE SAYS YOU HEAR IN A TORNADO."**

A storm chaser took this image of the tornado just before it moved into Joplin, Missouri.

"I started hearing that sound (like a train) and feeling the pressure change." KURTIS COX

Kurtis Cox

Kurtis Cox and his family had been celebrating his son's graduation when he saw threatening clouds. The family reached their basement just as the tornado hit.

"I JUST TOOK A LOOK AND SOMETHING JUST DIDN'T LOOK RIGHT," Cox said of the sky. "I could tell that there was something going on. I started hearing that sound (like a train) and feeling the pressure change."

"It seemed like it took forever for it to pass, and we could hear glass breaking and things hitting the house," he said. "When it was over, our basement was pretty much intact. Obviously when we got upstairs, it was a big shock."

An EF5 tornado moves through Joplin on May 22, 2011.

Terrla Cruse

Terrla Cruse was at home when the **tornado warning** sirens sounded. Most of the family got to the basement just before the tornado hit. They heard the roar and felt their house shake under the tornado's wrath. The Cruse family's home was destroyed. "Everything was gone," said Cruse, "our house, the whole neighborhood, just gone." Their 13-year-old cat, Lavern, was also missing.

For several days they searched through the rubble of their home. They hoped to recover some of their belongings and maybe find Lavern. "We decided to go back one more time," said Cruse. Suddenly, she heard meowing under the debris and began digging. When she saw Lavern, "It was shock and happiness." Lavern was thin and thirsty, but alive.

∧ Terrla Cruse is overjoyed after discovering her cat, Lavern, is alive after being trapped for 16 days in the rubble.

∨ The front stairs are the only part of the Cruse home intact after the tornado.

Rebuilding Joplin

"We only had to use it once, but it saved our lives." SHIRLEY CONNER

Don and Shirley Conner stand next to their storm shelter.

Shirley and Don Conner

"THESE WERE THE HOMES OF OUR NEIGHBORS AND OUR FRIENDS. WE LOST SOME GOOD NEIGHBORS," Shirley Conner said.

Shirley and her husband, Don, survived the storm by seeking shelter in a small crawlspace they had built under their bedroom. Most of the homes in Joplin don't have basements. Basements are expensive and difficult to build in Joplin because the ground is wet and rocky.

Much of Joplin had to be rebuilt after the tornado. Basements and storm shelters are now being built to protect people in future tornadoes. These shelters can even be closets built with reinforced steel walls and doors. Storm shelters are designed to withstand strong winds and flying debris that can cause damage or injury during a tornado.

This community experienced a lot of sadness because of this tragedy, but the people in Joplin are planning for the future. More storm shelters are being built and emergency plans are being made. The next time the severe weather warnings are issued, the people of Joplin will be ready.

Tornado damage is evident immediately after the tornado (top photo). Progress in clean up and repair is evident in the same place a few weeks later (lower photo).

One year after the tornado, the area below looks much different from May 23, 2011.

Roll Off Service

Check In What are some things you could do to prepare for a tornado?

GENRE Interview   **Read to find out** about Tim Samaras's tornado research.

TIM SAMARAS
SEVERE STORMS RESEARCHER

by Christopher Siegel

After deploying his tornado measuring device, Tim quickly photographs the oncoming storm.

"We thought we were following the storm. But then, when we looked up... we saw that the storm was headed straight for us! Talk about motivation! There is nothing more motivating to get up and go than the deadly force of a tornado headed straight for you! We moved faster that day than ever before!"

TIM SAMARAS, SEVERE STORMS RESEARCHER AND NATIONAL GEOGRAPHIC EXPLORER

Tim Samaras chased storms. Sometimes the storms chased him! Tim and the Tactical Weather Instrumented Sampling in or near Tornadoes Experiment (TWISTEX) team were tracking a tornado in Tornado Alley. They watched as the tornado changed course and headed directly for them. The team quickly released a tornado measuring device and then quickly drove away.

Identifying and Describing the Problem

National Geographic: What inspired you to study severe storms, specifically tornadoes?

Tim Samaras: It all started when I was about six years old and I saw the fantastic tornado in *The Wizard of Oz.* In the movie, the whirling, twisting tornado picked up the entire house—Dorothy and Toto, included! I became fascinated with tornadoes from then on. Later in life, I began to chase storms in Tornado Alley. Now, studying severe storms is my passion. I find each new storm to be as fascinating as the first.

Tim Samaras tracks an oncoming storm from the inside of the TWISTEX truck.

Why do you study tornadoes?

Tim Samaras: Tornadoes are fascinating, but dangerous. They don't just pick up houses and drop them off in the merry old Land of Oz. Tornadoes cause destruction. People lose their homes, sometimes their lives. I'm saddened when this happens. So I want to study tornadoes and research ways to help people better prepare before a storm hits.

When we know more about tornadoes, we will be able to make more accurate warnings. Right now, there are too many false alarms. This makes people less likely to seek shelter. Current warnings only average a slim 13 minutes. By understanding tornadoes better, we can warn people earlier. Every additional second of warning can save lives.

Engineering Solutions

National Geographic: In what ways do you use engineering skills in your research?

Tim Samaras: There isn't any tool or measuring device you can buy at the store to take measurements inside a tornado. So I use engineering skills to design weather instruments, such as the Turtle. So having the know-how and skills to build devices to measure storm activity is central to my work.

Tim uses engineering skills to develop research tools. These drawings show Tim's work in designing the Turtle.

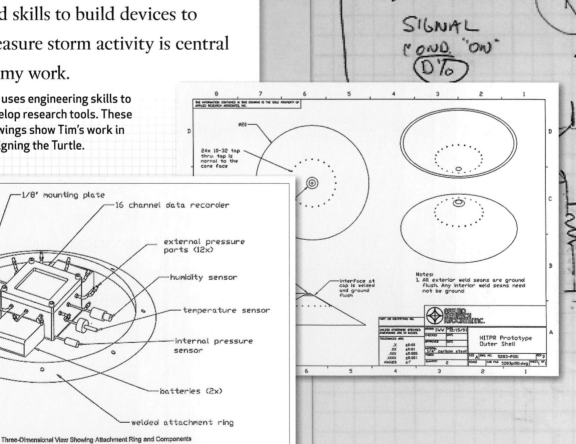

- 1/8" mounting plate
- 16 channel data recorder
- external pressure ports (12x)
- humidity sensor
- temperature sensor
- internal pressure sensor
- batteries (2x)
- welded attachment ring

Three-Dimensional View Showing Attachment Ring and Components

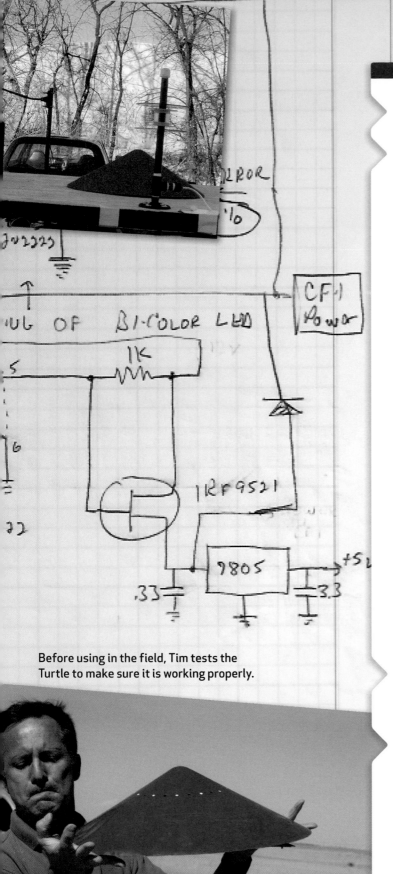

Before using in the field, Tim tests the Turtle to make sure it is working properly.

ΠG: What is the Turtle?

Tim Samaras: The Turtle is the name of the tornado measuring device I developed when I began my research. The outside cover that protects the device looks like the shell of a turtle, but it's red. Inside there are tools to measure wind speed and direction, air pressure, and other elements of a storm. There is also a video camera to take pictures inside a tornado. Technology is an important part of my research. Together, all these tools collect the data I need to better understand storms and how tornadoes develop.

ΠG: What can students do to develop engineering skills?

Tim Samaras: The best thing to do is to take science and math classes in school. These will help you learn the skills needed for engineering. Also, ask questions about how things are made. Be creative! Think about new ways to solve problems.

Designing and Improving Solutions

National Geographic: Could you describe how your ideas have changed and improved?

Tim Samaras: Take a look at my truck. It looks like a vehicle ready to explore Mars. My truck and all the tools attached to it are a product of the development of my ideas. Each new tool represents a new idea that has changed over all the years I've been researching storms.

The advancement of technology plays a big part in designing better instruments and finding new scientific information. If you can believe it, I once traveled across Tornado Alley without even a mobile phone! Now the inside of my truck looks more like the cockpit of an airplane than a normal truck.

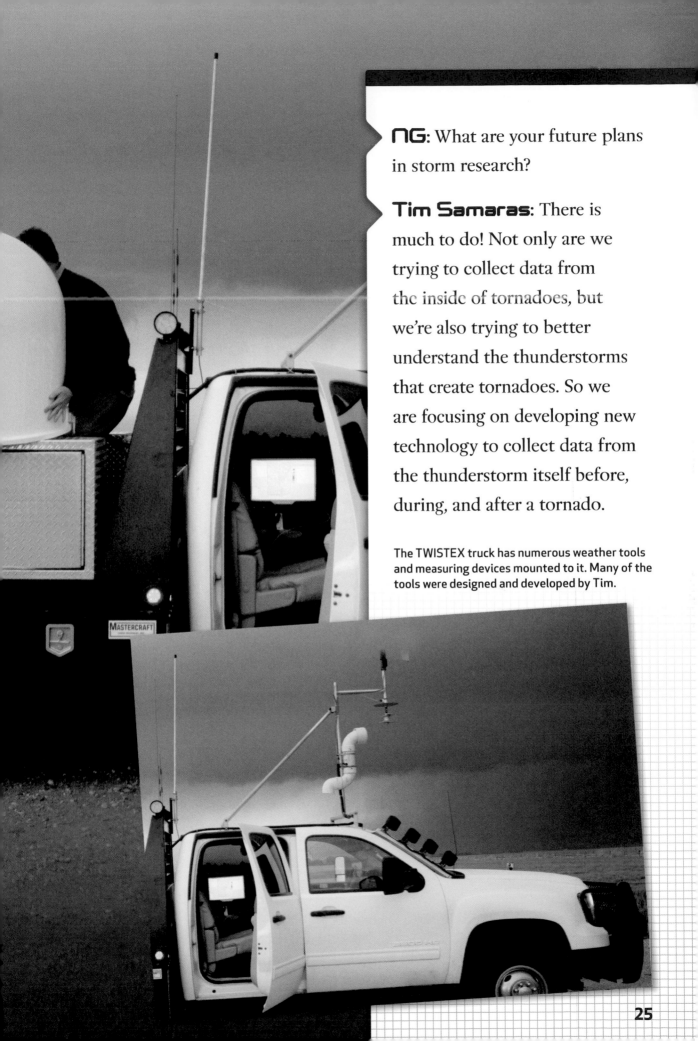

∩G: What are your future plans in storm research?

Tim Samaras: There is much to do! Not only are we trying to collect data from the inside of tornadoes, but we're also trying to better understand the thunderstorms that create tornadoes. So we are focusing on developing new technology to collect data from the thunderstorm itself before, during, and after a tornado.

The TWISTEX truck has numerous weather tools and measuring devices mounted to it. Many of the tools were designed and developed by Tim.

Results

National Geographic:
What do you do with the data
you collect about storms?

Tim Samaras: The data I
collect is only a small piece of
the puzzle. Hopefully, it will
add to our understanding of
tornadoes, but I don't work
alone. There are many other
scientists working to understand
how tornadoes form. It takes the
hard work of all these scientists
to find solutions so we can
improve our ability to forecast
tornadoes quickly. Scientists
share their findings by publishing
scientific papers for other
scientists to review and discuss.
This process is called **peer
review.** Sometimes the work of
one scientist will inspire others
to develop new experiments,
collect new data, and maybe find
a new solution. Science really can
be exciting!

NG: What would you suggest to students who are interested in severe weather?

Tim Samaras: Learn as much as you can about weather. There are many colleges and universities that have active tornado research programs that allow students to participate at all levels. Most of all, keep your focus on what you want to do! Sometimes schoolwork can become very difficult. Keep at it, and you will do great!

Tim tracks oncoming storms from satellite maps inside the TWISTEX truck. The outside of the truck has a variety of weather-measuring devices to record changes in the storms.

As a severe storms researcher, Tim Samaras made many new discoveries about tornadoes. He also wanted very much to inspire students just like you to study science and do scientific research. Through Tim's work, he believed he could inspire the next severe storms researcher. Perhaps that person is you!

Check In What other questions would you ask a severe storms researcher?

TIM'S TIPS FOR STAYING SAFE

by Tim Samaras

The most important part of my job as a severe storm researcher is to help people stay safe from severe storms, such as tornadoes. By collecting more data about tornadoes, I hope to be able to give earlier and more accurate warnings. Many more lives will be saved if more warning time is given before a tornado actually strikes.

Do you know the difference between a **tornado watch** and a **tornado warning**?

TORNADO WATCH

A TORNADO WATCH means weather conditions are right for a tornado to form in your area. Watch for signs of a tornado and be alert in case a tornado warning is issued.

TORNADO WARNING

A TORNADO WARNING means a tornado has been sighted and you may be in danger. When a warning is given, seek shelter immediately!

DURING A TORNADO

Have a plan and practice it with your family. If you have a storm shelter, use it. If not, follow these steps.

IF THERE IS A BASEMENT in the building you're in, go there. A basement is one of the safest places you can be during a tornado. Get under a heavy piece of furniture.

IF THERE ISN'T A BASEMENT, go to a bathroom or other room without windows on the lowest level of the building. If there is a bathtub, get inside it. Protect your head with your arms.

IF YOU'RE IN A MOBILE HOME, get out and seek shelter in a permanent building. Most mobile home parks have a tornado shelter. Know where the shelter is and go there immediately!

IF YOU'RE IN YOUR CAR OR OUTSIDE, do not try to outdrive or outrun a tornado. Seek shelter in a permanent building. If you are in an open area with no shelter, seek shelter in a ditch or other low area.

When you hear a tornado warning, you need to take action. Following the rights steps may just save your life.

Underground storm shelters are common in some areas of the United States, especially throughout Tornado Alley. Such underground shelters provide protection from tornadoes and other severe storms.

Check In Describe the steps you should follow to stay safe from a tornado.

Discuss

1. How does the information you read about in the interview with Tim Samaras relate to the other selections?

2. What new ideas or concepts about tornadoes did you learn about from this book?

3. In what ways do you think science, technology, engineering, and math are related in understanding severe storms better?

4. What are some things you could do to stay safe in the event of a tornado?

5. What other questions do you have about tornadoes? Where could you find answers to your questions?